AVITC

Birds of the Hawaiian Islands

Wolfgang J. Daunicht

AVITOPIA, Prof. Dr. Wolfgang J. Daunicht
Max-Born-Straße 12, D-60438 Frankfurt am Main
Telefax: +49(69)90756638
E-Mail: admin@avitopia.de

Further information is available at

www.avitopia.net

Table of Contents

4

Preface

The Hawaiian Islands are located in the Pacific Ocean. Legally the Hawaiian Islands belong to USA.

The Hawaiian Islands have a unique avifauna, with their endemic specialties, seabirds and large numbers of introduced species. Unfortunately, there are far more introduced species than surviving endemic species. Oahu, where the capital Honolulu is located, has relative few endemic bird species and the largest variety of introduced species. On Maui there is Haleakala National Park, while the Hawaii Volcanoes National Park is located on the 'Big Island'. Both are worth visiting not only because of the spectacular landscape, but also to look for rare endemic bird species. Both parks belong to an International Biosphere Reserve and a World Heritage Site.

The assessment of the global conservation status of bird species uses the criteria of the Red List (IUCN) 2012.

Legend
△ Near threatened
▲ Vulnerable
▲ Endangered
▲ Critically endangered
▲ Extinct in the wild
▲ Data deficient
Ø Invalid taxon
† Extinct
ⓔ Picture of an endemic subspecies
▣ Link to video with audio
▢ Link to video
◀) Link to audio

This e-book is based on a request to the AVITOPIA Data Base the 15th January 2022.
The request profile was:

Primary language: English - Secondary language: unrestricted

Maximum number of pictures per species: 1

Content and illustration: all names, optimal illustration

Scientific system: Clements et al. 2017

Method of area selection: Menu tree

Name of area: Hawaiian Islands

Survival criterion: unrestricted

Selection of a taxon: all birds

Taxonomic depth: Species of Birds

Selection of activity/nest/portrait: unrestricted

Selection of plumage/egg(s): unrestricted

Selection of image technique: unrestricted

In the resulting PDF or ePub file, resp., all index and register entries are linked.

Bird Topography

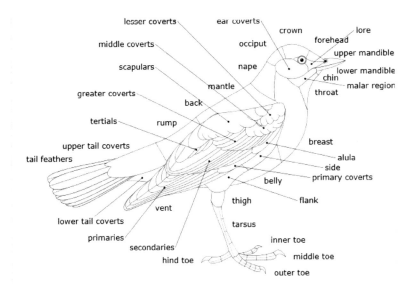

Species of Birds

Ducks and Geese - *Anatidae*

The family of Ducks and Geese occurs in all continents of the world except in Antarctica. The birds grow up to 30 - 180 cm long and live essentially on the water. The front three toes are webbed, the fourth toe is small and shifted upwards. All species swim, some dive well. Most species fly well, only a few are flightless. However, shortly after the breeding season, the birds adopt simple plumage and shed all flight feathers, so that they are unable to fly for some time. The nests are very diverse: there are nests on the ground, in ground caves, in steep walls and in tree hollows. The clutch comprises 4 to 12 eggs, the incubation lasts between 3 and 5 weeks and the young leave the nest soon after hatching.

Nene
de: Hawaiigans
fr: Bernache néné
es: Barnacla Nené
ja: ハワイガン
cn: 夏威夷黑雁
Branta sandvicensis
Endemic.
Vulnerable.

Photo G.Smart

♂♀ adult

Tundra Swan
de: Zwergschwan
fr: Cygne siffleur
es: Cisne Chico
ja: コハクチョウ
cn: 小天鹅
Cygnus columbianus

Photo W.D.G.Daunicht

adult

Blue-winged Teal
de: Blauflügelente
fr: Sarcelle à ailes bleues
es: Cerceta Aliazul
ja: ミカヅキシマアジ
cn: 蓝翅鸭
Spatula discors

Photo T.Koerner

♂ adult

Northern Shoveler
de: Löffelente
fr: Canard souchet
es: Cuchara Común
ja: ハシビロガモ
cn: 琵嘴鸭
Spatula clypeata

www.avitopia.net/bird.en/?vid=203010

♂ adult

Gadwall
de: Schnatterente
fr: Canard chipeau
es: Anade Friso
ja: オカヨシガモ
cn: 赤膀鸭
Mareca strepera

www.avitopia.net/bird.en/?vid=203101

♂ adult

American Wigeon
de: Nordamerikanische Pfeifente
fr: Canard d'Amérique
es: Silbón Americano
ja: アメリカヒドリ
cn: 绿眉鸭
Mareca americana

♂ adult

Laysan Duck
de: Laysanente
fr: Canard de Laysan
es: Ánade de Laysan
ja: レイサンマガモ
cn: 莱岛鸭
Anas laysanensis
Endemic.
Critically endangered.

♂ adult

FD Hawaiian Duck
de: Hawaiiente
fr: Canard des Hawaï
es: Ánade Hawaiano
ja: ハワイマガモ
cn: 夏威夷鸭
Anas wyvilliana
Endemic.
Endangered.

Photo R.Clapp

♂ adult

AU Mallard
de: Stockente
fr: Canard colvert
es: Ánade Real
ja: マガモ
cn: 绿头鸭
Anas platyrhynchos
Introduced.

Photo W.J.Daunicht

 www.avitopia.net/bird.en/?vid=203210
www.avitopia.net/bird.en/?aud=203210

♂ adult

PD Northern Pintail
de: Spießente
fr: Canard pilet
es: Ánade Rabudo
ja: オナガガモ
cn: 针尾鸭
Anas acuta

Photo D.Menke

www.avitopia.net/bird.en/?vid=203216

♂ adult

AU Green-winged Teal
de: Krickente
fr: Sarcelle d'hiver
es: Cerceta común
ja: コガモ
cn: 绿翅鸭
Anas crecca

Photo W.J.Daunicht

www.avitopia.net/bird.en/?vid=203219

Ring-necked Duck
 de: Ringschnabelente
 fr: Fuligule à collier
 es: Porrón Acollarado
 ja: クビワキンクロ
 cn: 环颈潜鸭
Aythya collaris

♂ adult

Greater Scaup
 de: Bergente
 fr: Fuligule milouinan
 es: Porrón Bastardo
 ja: スズガモ
 cn: 斑背潜鸭
Aythya marila

♂ adult

Lesser Scaup
 de: Kleine Bergente
 fr: Petit Fuligule
 es: Porrón Bola
 ja: コスズガモ
 cn: 小潜鸭
Aythya affinis

♂ adult

White-winged Scoter
 de: Samtente
 fr: Macreuse brune
 es: Negrón Especulado
 ja: ビロアドキンクロ
 cn: 斑脸海番鸭
Melanitta fusca
Vulnerable.

♂ adult

Common Goldeneye
de: Schellente
fr: Garrot à oeil d'or
es: Porrón Osculado
ja: ホオジロガモ
cn: 鹊鸭
Bucephala clangula

www.avitopia.net/bird.en/?vid=204502

♂ adult

New World Quails - *Odontophoridae*

The family of Old World Quails occurs mainly in America from southern Brazil to Canada, and two species of the family live in Africa. Their length ranges from 17 cm to 37 cm. They have short, strong legs, but they do not have a spur. They are diurnal ground birds that only fly in an emergency or to spend the night. They feed on animal and plant material alike. The nest is constructed on the ground. The clutches are between 3 to 15 eggs in size. The chicks are nidifuguous and quickly accompany their parents in large family groups.

California Quail
de: Schopfwachtel
fr: Colin de Californie
es: Colín de California
ja: カンムリウズラ
cn: 珠颈斑鹑
Callipepla californica
Introduced.

adult

Gambel's Quail
de: Helmwachtel
fr: Colin de Gambel
es: Colín de Gambel
ja: ズアカカンムリウズラ
cn: 黑腹翎鹑
Callipepla gambelii
Introduced.

adult

Pheasants - *Phasianidae*

The pheasant family is distributed worldwide, with the exception of northern Asia, southern South America and the polar regions. The lengths are very different and range from 13 cm to 2 m. They all have round wings, short necks and short thick beaks. The plumage is often very conspicuously patterned and the sexes are mostly different. Most pheasants live on the ground, but some species sleep in trees.

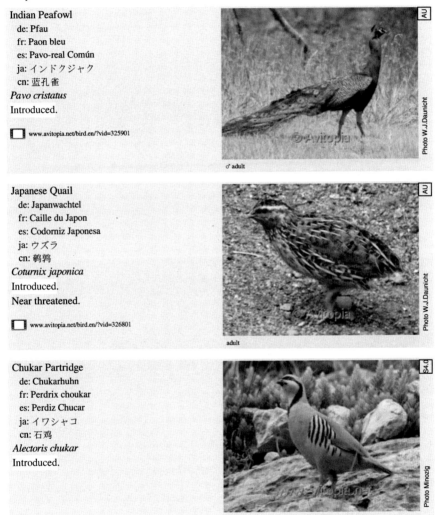

Indian Peafowl
  de: Pfau
  fr: Paon bleu
  es: Pavo-real Común
  ja: インドクジャク
  cn: 蓝孔雀
Pavo cristatus
Introduced.

www.avitopia.net/bird.en/?vid=325901

♂ adult

Photo W.J.Daunicht

Japanese Quail
  de: Japanwachtel
  fr: Caille du Japon
  es: Codorniz Japonesa
  ja: ウズラ
  cn: 鹌鹑
Coturnix japonica
Introduced.
Near threatened.

www.avitopia.net/bird.en/?vid=326801

adult

Photo W.J.Daunicht

Chukar Partridge
  de: Chukarhuhn
  fr: Perdrix choukar
  es: Perdiz Chucar
  ja: イワシャコ
  cn: 石鸡
Alectoris chukar
Introduced.

adult

Photo Minozig

adult

Drawing F.C.Vogel

PD **Erckel's Francolin**
de: Erckelfrankolin
fr: Francolin d'Erckel
es: Francolín de Erckel
ja: クロガオシャコ
cn: 棕顶鹧鸪
Pternistis erckelii
Introduced.

♂ adult

Photo W.J.Daunicht

AU **Black Francolin**
de: Halsbandfrankolin
fr: Francolin noir
es: Francolín Ventrinegro
ja: ムナグロシャコ
cn: 黑鹧鸪
Francolinus francolinus
Introduced.

adult

Photo J.Mosesso

PD **Grey Francolin**
de: Wachtelfrankolin
fr: Francolin gris
es: Francolín Gris
ja: シマシャコ
cn: 灰鹧鸪
Francolinus pondicerianus
Introduced.

♂ adult

Photo W.J.Daunicht

AU **Red Junglefowl**
de: Bankivahuhn
fr: Coq bankiva
es: Gallo Bankiva
ja: セキショクヤケイ
cn: 原鸡
Gallus gallus
Introduced.

www.avitopia.net/bird.en/?vid=327701
www.avitopia.net/bird.en/?aud=327701

Common Pheasant
de: Fasan
fr: Faisan de Colchide
es: Faisán Vulgar
ja: キジ
cn: 环颈雉
Phasianus colchicus
Introduced.

www.avitopia.net/bird.en/?vid=328701
www.avitopia.net/bird.en/?aud=328701

♂ adult

Kalij Pheasant
de: Kalifasan
fr: Faisan leucomèle
es: Faisán Kálij
ja: ミヤマハッカン
cn: 黑鹇
Lophura leucomelanos
Introduced.

www.avitopia.net/bird.en/?vid=329002

♂ adult

Wild Turkey
de: Truthuhn
fr: Dindon sauvage
es: Guajolote Gallipavo
ja: シチメンチョウ
cn: 火鸡
Meleagris gallopavo
Introduced.

♂ adult

Divers - *Gaviidae*

The species in the family of Loons occur in the higher latitudes of the northern hemisphere, however, they do migrate. They are between 65 cm and 95 cm long. They have small wings, webbed feet and powerful, pointed beaks. They can dive for up to 40 s, but they need a longer approach to take off. Their nests are always created on the shores of freshwater lakes. The young birds are led by both parents.

Black-throated Loon
de: Prachttaucher
fr: Plongeon arctique
es: Colimbo Ártico
ja: オオハム
cn: 黑喉潜鸟
Gavia arctica

breeding

Grebes - *Podicipedidae*

The family of Grebes are found on freshwater lakes around the world, except in the extreme north and south and on some islands. In winter they can also be found on the coast of the sea. The size ranges from 20 cm to 50 cm, the wings are short, tail feathers are missing. The toes have flap-like widenings. They only fly regularly and at night during the migration time. In addition, they are well adapted to aquatic life. Both parents lead the striped or spotted young birds until they become independent.

Horned Grebe
de: Ohrentaucher
fr: Grèbe esclavon
es: Zampullín Cuellirrojo
ja: ミミカイツブリ
cn: 角䴘
Podiceps auritus
Vulnerable.

breeding

Black-necked Grebe
  de: Schwarzhalstaucher
  fr: Grèbe à cou noir
  es: Zampullín Cuellinegro
  ja: ハジロカイツブリ
  cn: 黑颈䴙䴘
Podiceps nigricollis

breeding

Albatrosses - *Diomedeidae*

The family of Albatrosses lives in the oceans around the Antarctic up to 30 degrees southern latitude, only in the Pacific does the range extend to the Bering Sea to the north. Albatrosses are large, heavy birds with a body length of 70 cm to 135 cm. The wingspan can reach 370 cm, making it the largest among birds. The wings are long and narrow, the tail is short, and the feet are webbed. The strong hooked bill is covered with horn plates. Albatrosses form colonies on remote islands, where they prefer the wind side to be able to take off more easily. They have developed a special form of gliding, dynamic soaring. They land on the water to eat fish, octopus and other marine animals. They lay a single egg and some species take up to a year to fledge, so they can only raise young every two years. The chicks are altricial and are fed by both parents with regurgitated food.

Laysan Albatross
  de: Laysanalbatros
  fr: Albatros de Laysan
  es: Albatros de Laysan
  ja: コアホウドリ
  cn: 黑背信天翁
Phoebastria immutabilis
Near threatened.

adult, juvenile

Black-footed Albatross
  de: Schwarzfußalbatros
  fr: Albatros à pieds noirs
  es: Albatros Patinegro
  ja: クロアシアホウドリ
  cn: 黑脚信天翁
Phoebastria nigripes
Near threatened.

adult

adult

Short-tailed Albatross
de: Kurzschwanzalbatros
fr: Albatros à queue courte
es: Albatros Colicorto
ja: アホウドリ
cn: 短尾信天翁
Phoebastria albatrus
Vulnerable.

Photo R.Clapp

Petrels - *Procellariidae*

The family of Petrels is at home at sea all over the world. They essentially use the land for breeding, and some species even do so on the coast of Antarctica. Most of the species are migratory birds. The body length ranges from 30 cm to 90 cm. The birds have long, pointed wings and short tails, and their feet are webbed. The smaller species breed in caves or crevices, they defend the young birds by vomiting stinking oil.

adult

Kermadec Petrel
de: Kermadecsturmvogel
fr: Pétrel de Kermadec
es: Petrel de las Kermadec
ja: カワリシロハラミズナギドリ
cn: 克岛圆尾鹱
Pterodroma neglecta

Drawing J.G.Keulemans

adult

Herald Petrel
de: Wappen...
fr: Pétrel hérault
es: Petrel del Herald
ja: ヘラルドシロハラミズナギドリ
cn: 信使圆尾鹱
Pterodroma heraldica

Drawing J.G.Keulemans

Providence Petrel
  de: Solandersturmvogel
  fr: Pétrel de Solander
  es: Petrel de Solander
  ja: ハジロミズナギドリ
  cn: 棕头圆尾鹱
Pterodroma solandri
Vulnerable.

adult

Mottled Petrel
  de: Regensturmvogel
  fr: Pétrel maculé
  es: Petrel Moteado
  ja: マダラシロハラミズナギドリ
  cn: 鳞斑圆尾鹱
Pterodroma inexpectata
Near threatened.

adult

Juan Fernandez Petrel
  de: Salvinsturmvogel
  fr: Pétrel de Juan Fernandez
  es: Petrel de las Juan Fernández
  ja:
  ファンフェルナンデスシロハラミズナギドリ
  cn: 百颈圆尾鹱
Pterodroma externa
Vulnerable.

adult, pullus

Hawaiian Petrel
  de: Hawaiisturmvogel
  fr: Pétrel des Hawaï
  es: Petrel Hawaiano
  ja: ハワイシロハラミズナギドリ
  cn: 夏威夷圆尾鹱
Pterodroma sandwichensis
Breed-endemic.
Vulnerable.

adult

adult

[PD] Bonin Petrel
de: Boninsturmvogel
fr: Pétrel des Bonin
es: Petrel de las Bonin
ja: シロハラミズナギドリ
cn: 白额圆尾鹱
Pterodroma hypoleuca

adult

[PD] Black-winged Petrel
de: Schwarzflügel-Sturmvogel
fr: Pétrel à ailes noires
es: Petrel Alinegro
ja: ハグロシロハラミズナギドリ
cn: 黑翅圆尾鹱
Pterodroma nigripennis

adult

[PD] Cook's Petrel
de: Cooksturmvogel
fr: Pétrel de Cook
es: Petrel de Cook
ja: ハジロシロハラミズナギドリ
cn: 黑脚圆尾鹱
Pterodroma cookii
Vulnerable.

adult

[AU] Stejneger's Petrel
de: Stejnegersturmvogel
fr: Pétrel de Stejneger
es: Petrel de Más Afuera
ja: ヒメシロハラミズナギドリ
cn: 长嘴圆尾鹱
Pterodroma longirostris
Vulnerable.

Bulwer's Petrel
de: Bulwersturmvogel
fr: Pétrel de Bulwer
es: Petrel de Bulwer
ja: アナドリ
cn: 褐燕鸌
Bulweria bulwerii

adult

Black Petrel
de: Schwarzsturmvogel
fr: Puffin de Parkinson
es: Pardela de Parkinson
ja: クロミズナギドリ
cn: 黑风鸌
Procellaria parkinsoni
Vulnerable.

adult

Flesh-footed Shearwater
de: Blassfuß-Sturmtaucher
fr: Puffin à pieds pâles
es: Pardela Paticlara
ja: アカアシミズナギドリ
cn: 淡足鸌
Ardenna carneipes

adult

Wedge-tailed Shearwater
de: Keilschwanz-Sturmtaucher
fr: Puffin fouquet
es: Pardela del Pacífico
ja: オナガミズナギドリ
cn: 曳尾鸌
Ardenna pacifica

adult

adult

PD Buller's Shearwater
de: Graumantel-Sturmtaucher
fr: Puffin de Buller
es: Pardela Dorsigrís
ja: ミナミオナガミズナギドリ
cn: 灰背鹱
Ardenna bulleri

adult

PD Sooty Shearwater
de: Dunkler Sturmtaucher
fr: Puffin fuligineux
es: Pardela Sombría
ja: ハイイロミズナギドリ
cn: 灰鹱
Ardenna grisea
Near threatened.

adult

S3.d Short-tailed Shearwater
de: Kurzschwanz-Sturmtaucher
fr: Puffin à bec grêle
es: Pardela de Tasmania
ja: ハシボソミズナギドリ
cn: 短尾鹱
Ardenna tenuirostris

adult

PD Christmas Shearwater
de: Weihnachtssturmtaucher
fr: Puffin de la Nativité
es: Pardela de la Christmas
ja: コミズナギドリ
cn: 黑鹱
Puffinus nativitatis

Newell's Shearwater
  de: Newellsturmtaucher
  fr: Puffin de Newell
  es: Pardela de Newell
  ja: ハワイセグロミズナギドリ
  cn: 夏威夷鹱
Puffinus newelli
Breed-endemic.
Endangered.

adult

Storm-petrels - *Hydrobatidae*

The family of Storm-petrels is widespread on all oceans of the earth and occurs partly in large numbers. With a body length of 14 cm to 25 cm, they are the smallest seabirds with webbed feet. Your weak legs are hardly able to carry their body weight without the support of the wings. They breed in colonies in caves or crevices, which they usually only attend at night. Although they usually breed on mammal-free islands, the greatest danger comes from introduced mammals. The Guadalupe storm-petrel was driven to extinction by feral cats.

Wilson's Storm Petrel
  de: Buntfuß-Sturmschwalbe
  fr: Océanite de Wilson
  es: Paíño de Wilson
  ja: アシナガウミツバメ
  cn: 黄蹼洋海燕
Oceanites oceanicus

adult

Leach's Storm Petrel
  de: Wellenläufer
  fr: Océanite cul-blanc
  es: Paíño Boreal
  ja: コシジロウミツバメ
  cn: 白腰叉尾海燕
Oceanodroma leucorhoa

adult

adult

Drawing J.G.Keulemans

Band-rumped Storm Petrel
de: Madeirawellenläufer
fr: Océanite de Castro
es: Paíño de Madeira
ja: クロコシジロウミツバメ
cn: 斑腰叉尾海燕
Oceanodroma castro

adult

Photo unknown

Tristram's Storm Petrel
de: Tristramwellenläufer
fr: Océanite de Tristram
es: Paíño de Tristram
ja: オアストンウミツバメ
cn: 褐翅叉尾海燕
Oceanodroma tristrami
Near threatened.

Tropic-birds - *Phaethontidae*

The family of Tropicbirds occurs on all tropical oceans. With a length of 41 cm to 48 cm, they belong to the medium-sized birds. They have long, pointed wings and a wedge-shaped tail, the central feathers of which are greatly elongated. The legs are very short, the feet are webbed. The head is large with a strong, slightly curved bill. They fly quickly and pounce on small fish and octopus out of the air. They nest in large, heavily populated colonies on the ground or in a crevice. The young are altricial, are fed by both parents and only fledged after up to 15 weeks.

adult

Photo Sassi Fayon

White-tailed Tropicbird
de: Weißschwanz-Tropikvogel
fr: Phaéton à bec jaune
es: Rabijunco Menor
ja: シラオネッタイチョウ
cn: 白尾鹲
Phaethon lepturus

Red-tailed Tropicbird
  de: Rotschwanz-Tropikvogel
  fr: Phaéton à brins rouges
  es: Rabijunco Colirrojo
  ja: アカオネッタイチョウ
  cn: 红尾鹲
Phaethon rubricauda

♂♀ adult

Frigate-birds - *Fregatidae*

The family of Frigate-birds can be found at all tropical and subtropical seas. Their length ranges from 80 cm to 105 cm. They have very long wings, a curved beak, and a forked tail. The males have a scarlet throat pouch during the breeding season, which is inflated during courtship. They feed on fish, but never go down on the water, instead catch them in flight. Frigate birds often parasitize other birds by chasing them until they regurgitate their food. The nest can reach a diameter of 4.5 m. The single egg is incubated by both adult birds for 40 days. The chick is fledged after 4 to 5 months.

Great Frigatebird
  de: Bindenfregattvogel
  fr: Frégate du Pacifique
  es: Rabihorcado Grande
  ja: オオグンカンドリ
  cn: 黑腹军舰鸟
Fregata minor

♂ adult

Gannets, Boobies - *Sulidae*

The family of Boobies is common on all seas near the coast. The birds are 65 cm to 100 cm long. The wings are long and pointed, the legs are short and the feet are large and webbed. The beak is strong and has no nostrils. Boobies are extremely elegant fliers, but quite awkward on the ground. They hunt fish for which they plunge into water from a height of up to 35 m in order to pursue them under water and to grab them with their beak. They breed in colonies on the ground or on trees. The young birds are provided with regurgitated food.

Masked Booby
de: Maskentölpel
fr: Fou masqué
es: Alcatraz Enmascarado
ja: アオツラカツオドリ
cn: 蓝脸鲣鸟
Sula dactylatra

Photo R.Graf

adult

Brown Booby
de: Weißbauchtölpel
fr: Fou brun
es: Piquero Pardo
ja: カツオドリ
cn: 褐鲣鸟
Sula leucogaster

Photo D.Patte

adult

Red-footed Booby
de: Rotfußtölpel
fr: Fou à pieds rouges
es: Piquero Patirrojo
ja: アカアシカツオドリ
cn: 红脚鲣鸟
Sula sula

Photo Charlesjsharp

♂ adult

Herons - *Ardeidae*

The heron family of Herons occurs on all continents and on many islands. The body length ranges from 28 nm to 140 cm. The wings are large, the tail is short. Legs, toes and neck are long, the latter has a characteristic S-shape. They feed mainly on fish, but also eat other small animals. They mostly breed in colonies. The food brought in is regurgitated in front of the chicks.

Cattle Egret
de: Kuhreiher
fr: Héron garde-boeufs
es: Garcilla Bueyera
ja: アマサギ
cn: 牛背鹭
Bubulcus ibis

Introduced.

www.avitopia.net/bird.en/?vid=750901

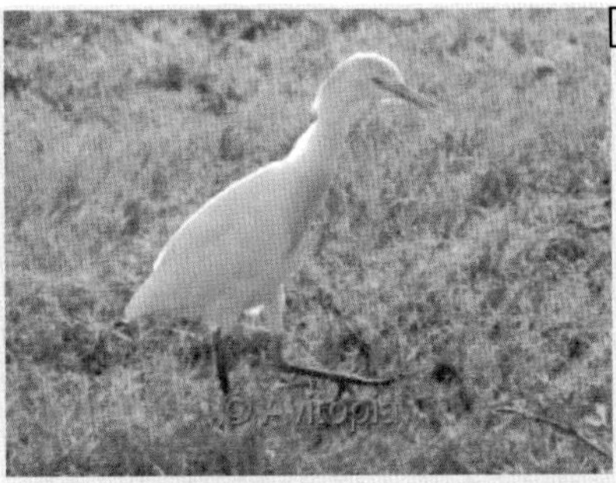

AU

breeding

Photo W.J.Daunicht

Black-crowned Night Heron
de: Nachtreiher
fr: Bihoreau gris
es: Martinete Común
ja: ゴイサギ
cn: 夜鹭
Nycticorax nycticorax

www.avitopia.net/bird.en/?vid=751501

AU

breeding

Photo W.J.Daunicht

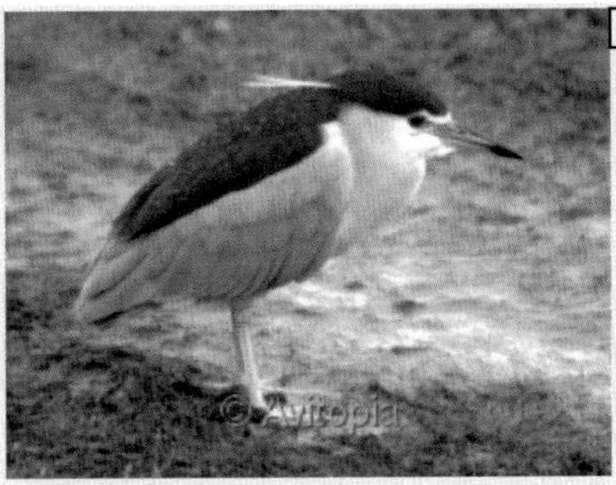

Birds of Prey - *Accipitridae*

The family of Birds of Prey is found worldwide with the exception of the Arctic, Antarctic and most of the oceanic islands. Birds of Prey are of various sizes (20 - 115 cm), they have long, round wings, curved claws and a short hooked bill. The sexes are almost the same, the female is almost always larger. All species are good fliers, and many sail well too. They mainly hunt live animals, only the vultures are scavengers. Even fishing species are among them.

adult

PD Golden Eagle
 de: Steinadler
 fr: Aigle royal
 es: Águila Real
 ja: イヌワシ
 cn: 金雕
Aquila chrysaetos

www.avitopia.net/bird.en/?vid=879106

adult

PD Sharp-shinned Hawk
 de: Eckschwanzsperber
 fr: Épervier brun
 es: Azor Rojizo
 ja: アシボソハイタカ
 cn: 纹腹鹰
Accipiter striatus

adult

PD Hawaiian Hawk
 de: Hawaiibussard
 fr: Buse d'Hawaï
 es: Busardo Hawaiano
 ja: ハワイノスリ
 cn: 夏威夷鵟
Buteo solitarius
Endemic.
Near threatened.

Rails, Waterhens, and Coots - *Rallidae*

The family of Rails and Coots occurs worldwide except in the polar regions. Rails are at most medium-sized birds (15 - 50 cm) with short wings and very short tails. The toes are long and have swimming lobes in the coots. The sexes usually look the same. Almost all species swim well. Many only become active at dusk or are night birds. Some are able to fly long distances, while island species are partially flightless.

Buff-banded Rail
  de: Bindenralle
  fr: Râle tiklin
  es: Rascón Filipino
  ja: ナンヨウクイナ
  cn: 红眼斑秧鸡
Gallirallus philippensis

adult

Laysan Crake
  de: Laysansumpfhuhn
  fr: Marouette de Laysan
  es: Polluela de Laysan
  ja: レイサンクイナ
  cn: 雷仙岛秧鸡
Zapornia palmeri †
Endemic.
Last seen 1944.

♂ adult

Hawaiian Crake
  de: Hawaiisumpfhuhn
  fr: Marouette des Hawaï
  es: Polluela Hawaiana
  ja: ハワイクイナ
  cn: 夏威夷秧鸡
Zapornia sandwichensis †
Endemic.
Last seen 1844.

adult

AU | Common Gallinule
de: Amerikanisches Teichhuhn
fr: Gallinule d'Amérique
es: Gallineta americana
ja: アメリカバン
cn: 黑水鸡
Gallinula galeata

adult

PD | Hawaiian Coot
de: Hawaiiblässhuhn
fr: Foulque des Hawaï
es: Focha Hawaiana
ja: ハワイオオバン
cn: 夏威夷骨顶
Fulica alai
Endemic.
Vulnerable.

adult

Stilts and Avocets - *Recurvirostridae*

The family of Stilts and Avocets is widespread worldwide; the northern populations are migratory birds. The body length is 30 cm to 50 cm. They have very long legs and a thin beak that is straight or curved upwards. They fly well and can swim well. They search the mud in shallow waters for invertebrates. They nest in colonies, the nest-fleeing young birds are looked after by both parents. The defense of the offspring includes various distraction techniques from simulating a 'broken wing' to 'false brooding' in full view of a predator.

PB | Black-necked Stilt
de: Schwarznacken-Stelzenläufer
fr: Échasse d'Amérique
es: Cigüeñuela de Cuello Negro
ja: クロエリセイタカシギ
cn: 黑颈长脚鹬
Himantopus mexicanus

www.avitopia.net/bird.en/?vid=1250104

adult

Oystercatcher - *Haematopodidae*

The family of oystercatchers is found in temperate and tropical waters from Iceland and the Aleutian Islands to Cape Horn and Tasmania. The body length of the medium-sized birds is 32 cm to 45 cm. The legs are long and strong, the feet have small webs. The beak is long, strong and compressed at the sides. Their diet consists of mussels, crabs, worms and insects, but oysters are not the main ingredient. Outside of the breeding season, they are sociable and then gather in large flocks that can reach a few thousand. The chicks who flee the nest are looked after by both parents until they have fledged after five weeks.

American Oystercatcher
   de: Braunmantel-Austernfischer
   fr: Huîtrier d'Amérique
   es: Ostrero Pío Americano
   ja: アメリカミヤコドリ
   cn: 美洲蛎鹬
Haematopus palliatus

adult

Plovers - *Charadriidae*

The plover family is global; many species are migratory birds. The body length ranges from 15 cm to 40 cm. Plover have a stocky body and long wings, the hind toe is receded or missing completely. They are ground birds that can run quickly, but also fly very well and quickly. In the vicinity of the nest or the young birds, the adult birds use seduction by simulating a broken wing and luring away a dangerous animal.

Grey Plover
   de: Kiebitzregenpfeifer
   fr: Pluvier argenté
   es: Chorlito Gris
   ja: ダイゼン
   cn: 灰鸻
Pluvialis squatarola

breeding

PD Pacific Golden Plover
   de: Pazifischer Goldregenpfeifer
   fr: Pluvier fauve
   es: Chorlito Dorado Siberiano
   ja: アジアムナグロ
   cn: 金鸻
   Pluvialis fulva

Photo O.W.Johnson

breeding

Sandpipers and Snipes - *Scolopacidae*

The family of Snipes is distributed worldwide, most of the species are migratory birds that sometimes cover great distances. The body length ranges from 13 cm to 60 cm. They usually live near water and outside the breeding season often form large flocks on the seashore. The diet consists of small invertebrates. The young birds leave the nest immediately after hatching.

PD Bristle-thighed Curlew
   de: Borstenbrachvogel
   fr: Courlis d'Alaska
   es: Zarapito del Pacífico
   ja: ハリモモチュウシャクシギ
   cn: 太平洋杓鹬
   Numenius tahitiensis
   Vulnerable.

Photo G.Kramer

adult

AU Whimbrel
   de: Regenbrachvogel
   fr: Courlis corlieu
   es: Zarapito Trinador
   ja: チュウシャクシギ
   cn: 中杓鹬
   Numenius phaeopus

www.avitopia.net/bird.en/?vid=1450202

Photo W.J.Daunicht

adult

Bar-tailed Godwit
  de: Pfuhlschnepfe
  fr: Barge rousse
  es: Aguja Colipinta
  ja: オオソリハシシギ
  cn: 斑尾塍鹬
Limosa lapponica
Near threatened.

www.avitopia.net/bird.en/?vid=1450301

breeding

Ruddy Turnstone
  de: Steinwälzer
  fr: Tournepierre à collier
  es: Vuelvepiedras Común
  ja: キョウジョシギ
  cn: 翻石鹬
Arenaria interpres

breeding

Red Knot
  de: Knutt
  fr: Bécasseau maubèche
  es: Correlimos Gordo
  ja: コオバシギ
  cn: 红腹滨鹬
Calidris canutus
Near threatened.

breeding

Sharp-tailed Sandpiper
  de: Spitzschwanz-Strandläufer
  fr: Bécasseau à queue pointue
  es: Correlimos Acuminado
  ja: ウズラシギ
  cn: 尖尾滨鹬
Calidris acuminata

breeding

non-breeding

Photo W.J.Daunicht

AU **Sanderling**
  de: Sanderling
  fr: Bécasseau sanderling
  es: Correlimos Tridáctilo
  ja: ミユビシギ
  cn: 三趾滨鹬
  Calidris alba

breeding

Photo T.Bowman

PD **Dunlin**
  de: Alpenstrandläufer
  fr: Bécasseau variable
  es: Correlimos Común
  ja: ハマシギ
  cn: 黑腹滨鹬
  Calidris alpina

breeding

Photo W.D.G.Daunicht

LIC **Pectoral Sandpiper**
  de: Graubrust-Strandläufer
  fr: Bécasseau à poitrine cendrée
  es: Correlimos Pectoral
  ja: アメリカウズラシギ
  cn: 斑胸滨鹬
  Calidris melanotos

breeding

Photo T.Bowman

PD **Long-billed Dowitcher**
  de: Großer Schlammläufer
  fr: Bécassin à long bec
  es: Agujeta Escolopácea
  ja: オオハシシギ
  cn: 长嘴半蹼鹬
  Limnodromus scolopaceus

Wilson's Snipe

de: Amerikanische Bekassine
fr: Bécassine de Wilson
es: Becasina
ja: アメリカシギ
cn: 美洲沙锥
Gallinago delicata

adult

Grey-tailed Tattler

de: Grauschwanz-Wasserläufer
fr: Chevalier de Sibérie
es: Playero Siberiano
ja: キアシシギ
cn: 灰尾漂鹬
Tringa brevipes
Near threatened.

breeding

Wandering Tattler

de: Wanderwasserläufer
fr: Chevalier errant
es: Playero de Alaska
ja: メリケンキアシシギ
cn: 漂鹬
Tringa incana

non-breeding

Lesser Yellowlegs

de: Kleiner Gelbschenkel
fr: Petit Chevalier
es: Archibebe Patigualdo Chico
ja: コキアシシギ
cn: 小黄脚鹬
Tringa flavipes

adult

Jaegers - *Stercorariidae*

The family of Jaegers is native to the arctic and subarctic areas of the northern and southern hemispheres. They migrate very far and can spend indefinite time at sea. The body length ranges from 40 cm to 60 cm. Their feet are webbed and have strong claws. The beak is strong and has a curved tip. Skuas are very fast and agile fliers. They breed near bird colonies and are aggressive predators and parasites there. They chase other birds until they vomit their food.

adult

PD South Polar Skua
de: Antarktikskua
fr: Labbe de McCormick
es: Págalo Polar
ja: ナンキョクオオトウゾクカモメ
cn: 灰贼鸥
Stercorarius maccormicki

Drawing J.Smit

adult

PD Pomarine Jaeger
de: Spatelraubmöwe
fr: Labbe pomarin
es: Págalo Pomarino
ja: トウゾクカモメ
cn: 中贼鸥
Stercorarius pomarinus

Drawing J.G.Keulemans

adult, dark phase

AU Parasitic Jaeger
de: Schmarotzerraubmöwe
fr: Labbe parasite
es: Págalo Parásito
ja: クロトウゾクカモメ
cn: 短尾贼鸥
Stercorarius parasiticus

Photo W.J.Daunicht

Long-tailed Jaeger
  de: Falkenraubmöwe
  fr: Labbe à longue queue
  es: Págalo Rabero
  ja: シロハラトウゾクカモメ
  cn: 长尾贼鸥
Stercorarius longicaudus

adult

Auks - *Alcidae*

The family of Auks can be found throughout the Arctic region, the North Atlantic and the North Pacific. Their body length ranges from 17 cm to 70 cm. They are clumsy birds with short wings, feet and tails. Alks come ashore only to breed, all swim and dive well, but do not fly well. They mainly eat fish, which they chase with flapping wings underwater. They breed on ledges, in caves or niches.

Ancient Murrelet
  de: Silberalk
  fr: Guillemot à cou blanc
  es: Mérgulo Antiguo
  ja: ウミスズメ
  cn: 扁嘴海雀
Synthliboramphus antiquus

breeding, non-breeding

Gulls - *Laridae*

The family of Gulls is found worldwide, most of the species are migratory birds. The body length ranges from 20 cm to 75 cm. Gulls are strongly built, they have long, pointed wings and a rather long tail. Their feet are webbed. They are very good fliers who often sail or glide. They can also swim well, but few species dive. They often breed in large colonies.

breeding

AU | Laughing Gull
  de: Aztekenmöwe
  fr: Mouette atricille
  es: Gaviota Guanaguanare
  ja: ワライカモメ
  cn: 笑鸥
  Leucophaeus atricilla

Photo W.J.Daunicht

breeding

S4.0 | Franklin's Gull
  de: Präriemöwe
  fr: Mouette de Franklin
  es: Gaviota Pipizcan
  ja: アメリカズグロカモメ
  cn: 弗氏鸥
  Leucophaeus pipixcan

Photo D.Gordon E.Robertson

adult

AU | Ring-billed Gull
  de: Ringschnabelmöwe
  fr: Goéland à bec cerclé
  es: Gaviota de Delaware
  ja: クロワカモメ
  cn: 环嘴鸥
  Larus delawarensis

Photo W.J.Daunicht

Herring Gull
  de: Silbermöwe
  fr: Goéland argenté
  es: Gaviota Argéntea
  ja: セグロカモメ
  cn: 银鸥
Larus argentatus

breeding

Glaucous-winged Gull
  de: Beringmöwe
  fr: Goéland à ailes grises
  es: Gaviota de Bering
  ja: ワシカモメ
  cn: 灰翅鸥
Larus glaucescens

adult

Brown Noddy
  de: Noddi
  fr: Noddi brun
  es: Tiñosa Boba
  ja: クロアジサシ
  cn: 白顶玄燕鸥
Anous stolidus

adult

Black Noddy
  de: Weißkopfnoddi
  fr: Noddi noir
  es: Tiñosa Menuda
  ja: ヒメクロアジサシ
  cn: 玄燕鸥
Anous minutus

adult

Photo Duncan Wright

adult

Blue Noddy
de: Blaunoddi
fr: Noddi bleu
es: Tiñosa Azulada
ja: ハイイロアジサシ
cn: 蓝灰燕鸥
Anous ceruleus

Photo R.Hagerty

adult

Angel Tern
de: Feenseeschwalbe
fr: Gygis blanche
es: Charrán Blanco
ja: シロアジサシ
cn: 白燕鸥
Gygis alba

Photo Sassi Fayon

adult, Egg(s)

Sooty Tern
de: Rußseeschwalbe
fr: Sterne fuligineuse
es: Charrán Sombrío
ja: セグロアジサシ
cn: 乌燕鸥
Onychoprion fuscatus

Drawing J.G.Keulemans

adult, juvenile

Spectacled Tern
de: Brillenseeschwalbe
fr: Stern à dos gris
es: Charrán Lunado
ja: ナンヨウマミジロアジサシ
cn: 灰背燕鸥
Onychoprion lunatus

Little Tern
  de: Zwergseeschwalbe
  fr: Sterne naine
  es: Charrancito Común
  ja: コアジサシ
  cn: 白额燕鸥
Sternula albifrons

breeding

Least Tern
  de: Amerikanische Zwergseeschwalbe
  fr: Petite Sterne
  es: Charrancito Americano
  ja: アメリカコアジサシ
  cn: 小白额燕鸥
Sternula antillarum

adult

Black-naped Tern
  de: Schwarznacken-Seeschwalbe
  fr: Sterne diamant
  es: Charrán de Sumatra
  ja: エリグロアジサシ
  cn: 黑枕燕鸥
Sterna sumatrana

adult

Arctic Tern
  de: Küstenseeschwalbe
  fr: Sterne arctique
  es: Charrán Artico
  ja: キョクアジサシ
  cn: 北极燕鸥
Sterna paradisaea

breeding

AU | Swift Tern
de: Eilseeschwalbe
fr: Sterne huppée
es: Charrán Piquigualdo
ja: オオアジサシ
cn: 大凤头燕鸥
Thalasseus bergii

Photo W.J.Daunicht

breeding

Sandgrouses - *Pteroclidae*

The family of Sandgrouses is found in Africa and Eurasia. The body length is 23 cm to 40 cm. They have pointed wings, the tail is long and pointed. The legs are short and have strong toes. Their habitat are steppes and semi-deserts, in which they live as ground birds. In several species, the males' abdominal plumage can absorb water so that it can be transported for kilometers to the nest in order to water the chicks.

PD | Chestnut-bellied Sandgrouse
de: Braunbauchflughuhn
fr: Ganga à ventre brun
es: Ganga Moruna
ja: チャバラサケイ
cn: 栗腹沙鸡
Pterocles exustus
Introduced.

Drawing Pretre

♂ adult

Pigeons and Doves - *Columbidae*

The family of Pigeons and Doves is found all over the world except in the coldest regions. The body lengths range from 15 cm to 84 cm. They have medium-sized wings and often a long tail. The beak is rather short and not strong. The sexes are mostly the same. Their diet is predominantly vegetarian. The naked young birds are fed 'pigeon milk', a secretion that is formed in the parents' goiter.

Common Pigeon
de: Felsentaube
fr: Pigeon biset
es: Paloma Bravía
ja: カワラバト(ドバト)
cn: 原鸽
Columba livia
Introduced.

www.avitopia.net/bird.en/?vid=1650101

adult

Spotted Dove
de: Perlhalstaube
fr: Tourterelle tigrine
es: Tórtola Moteada
ja: カノコバト
cn: 珠颈斑鸠
Streptopelia chinensis
Introduced.

♂♀ adult

Zebra Dove
de: Sperbertäubchen
fr: Géopélie zébrée
es: Tortolita Estriada
ja: チョウショウバト
cn: 斑姬地鸠
Geopelia striata
Introduced.

adult

PD Mourning Dove
de: Carolinataube
fr: Tourterelle triste
es: Zenaida Huilota
ja: ナゲキバト
cn: 哀鸽
Zenaida macroura
Introduced.

www.avitopia.net/bird.en/?vid=1652906

Photo D.Menke

adult

Barn owls - *Tytonidae*

The family of Barn Owls includes only a few species, but one of them is a true cosmopolitan. It occurs on all continents and only avoids the colder areas of the earth. The body length ranges from 23 cm to 55 cm. The legs are quite long, the central claw is comb-like. The head is endowed with a conspicuous veil and has a curved beak. Barn owls are nocturnal hunters that fly noiselessly near the ground. They can hear directionally and are able to locate their prey by hearing only.

AU Barn Owl
de: Schleiereule
fr: Effraie des clochers
es: Lechuza Común
ja: メンフクロウ
cn: 仓鸮
Tyto alba
Introduced.

www.avitopia.net/bird.en/?vid=1750112

Photo W.J.Daunicht

adult

Owls - *Strigidae*

The family of Owls is found worldwide. They have compact bodies (13 cm - 70 cm) and usually wide wings and rounded tails. The toes are strong, one of which is a turning toe that helps with grip. The head is large, the neck short. The eyes are directed rather forward, the beak is short and hook-shaped. Owls mainly hunt at night, benefiting from their noiseless flight and sharp hearing.

Short-eared Owl
  de: Sumpfohreule
  fr: Hibou des marais
  es: Búho Campestre
  ja: コミミズク
  cn: 短耳鸮
Asio flammeus

adult

Swifts - *Apodidae*

The family of Swifts is globally distributed except in the coldest regions. They are small birds, 9 cm to 23 cm long. The wings are long and pointed, the legs and feet are very small and the beak is small with a crooked point and a wide throat. Sails are perfectly adapted to life in the air, and some species are able to spend the night in flight and to mate. They are excellent and fast fliers, on the other hand, many species cannot take off from the ground. The nests of a few species are made entirely of saliva and are considered a delicacy in Chinese cuisine. Some species of salangan have the exceptional echolocation capability. They use this to orient themselves in underground cave systems, where their nesting sites are.

Mariana Swiftlet
  de: Marianensalangane
  fr: Salangane de Guam
  es: Salangana de Guam
  ja: ガムムジアナツバメ
  cn: 关岛金丝燕
Aerodramus bartschi
Introduced.
Endangered.

adult

Falcons - *Falconidae*

The family of Falcons is found on every continent except Antarctica. Their length ranges from 15 cm to 65 cm. Hawks have long, pointed wings, a half-length tail and short legs that end in long toes with curved claws. The beak is short and usually has a so-called 'falcon tooth' in the upper beak. The flight is determined and fast. Some species strike their prey in flight after a chase, while other species take them on the ground after diving. In fact, the fastest fliers among birds belong to this family.

Peregrine Falcon
de: Wanderfalke
fr: Faucon pèlerin
es: Halcón Peregrino
ja: ハヤブサ
cn: 游隼
Falco peregrinus

Photo S.Maslowski

adult

Old World Parrots - *Psittaculidae*

This family is limited to the warm areas of the 'Old World'. It consists of the five subfamilies Agapornithinae, Loriinae, Platycercinae, Psittacellinae and Psittaculinae. The body length ranges from 10 cm to 50 cm. The legs are short, two toes are pointing forward and two are pointing backward with strong claws. The beak is strong and strongly curved. They nest in hollows and less often in crevices.

Rose-ringed Parakeet
de: Halsbandsittich
fr: Perruche à collier
es: Cotorra de Kramer
ja: ホンセイインコ
cn: 红领绿鹦鹉
Psittacula krameri

Introduced.

www.avitopia.net/bird.en/?kom=2651103

Photo W.J.Daunicht

♂ adult

New World and African Parrots - *Psittacidae*

This family is limited to the continents of America and Africa. Most of the species in this family live in America, with only a few species in Africa. The size ranges from 12 cm to 100 cm. Many species have bright colors, caused by the Dyck textures in the feathers, in which incident light is refracted. Most of the species are cavity breeders.

Red-crowned Amazon
   de: Grünwangenamazone
   fr: Amazone à joues vertes
   es: Amazona Tamaulipeca
   ja: メキシコアカボウシインコ
   cn: 红冠鹦哥
Amazona viridigenalis
Introduced.
Endangered.

♂ adult

Mitred Parakeet
   de: Rotmaskensittich
   fr: Conure mitrée
   es: Aratinga Mitrada
   ja: ベニガオメキシコインコ
   cn: 红耳绿鹦哥
Psittacara mitratus
Introduced.

♂♀ adult

Red-masked Parakeet
   de: Guayaquilsittich
   fr: Conure à tête rouge
   es: Aratinga de Guayaquil
   ja: オナガアカボウシインコ
   cn: 红头鹦哥
Psittacara erythrogenys
Introduced.
Near threatened.

adult

Monarchs - *Monarchidae*

The family of Monarch-flycatchers are found in Africa, Asia, Australia and many islands in the Pacific. Most species live in the tropics, only a few extend into the temperate latitudes. Their body length ranges from 9 cm to 50 cm, including elongated tail feathers. They have wide, flat bills and stiff bristles near the nostrils. They are arborial birds and feed mainly on insects and small spiders. Their nests are usually built from plant material in a fork of a branch, only one species builds a mud nest. Some species decorate their nests with lichen.

S2.5 Elepaio
de: Elepaio
fr: Monarque élépaïo
es: Elepaio de Hawaii
ja: ハワイヒタキ
cn: 蚋鹟
Chasiempis sandwichensis
Endemic.
Endangered.

Photo Eike Wulfmeyer

♀ adult

PD Kauai Elepaio
de: Kauaimonarch
fr: Monarque de Kauai
es: Elepaio de Kauai
ja: カウアイヒタキ
cn: 考岛蚋鹟
Chasiempis sclateri
Endemic.
Vulnerable.

Drawing F.W.Frohawk

♂ adult

PD Oahu Elepaio
de: Oahumonarch
fr: Monarque d'Oahu
es: Elepaio de Oahu
ja: オアフヒタキ
cn: 瓦岛蚋鹟
Chasiempis ibidis
Endemic.
Endangered.

Drawing F.W.Frohawk

♂ adult

Ravens - *Corvidae*

The family of Ravens occurs worldwide with the exception of New Zealand and some islands. The body length is between 18 cm and 70 cm; so among them are the largest of all songbirds. Ravens have powerful bills and often hold the food with their feet when eating. They are curious and one of the most intelligent species in the entire bird world.

Hawaiian Crow
   de: Hawaiikrähe
   fr: Corneille d'Hawaï
   es: Cuervo Hawaiano
   ja: ハワイガラス
   cn: 夏威夷乌鸦
Corvus hawaiiensis
Endemic.
Extinct in the wild.

adult

Larks - *Alaudidae*

The family of Larks occurs all over the world with the exception of New Zealand and many islands. Larks are rather small birds (12 cm - 23 cm). In most species, the claw of the hind toe is long and pointed. They love open terrain and advance into the hottest deserts. They look for food on the ground and eat insects, snails, seeds and buds. The fluid requirement is often met from food. Some species protect their nest hollow on the windward side with a little stone wall. The chicks are looked after by both parents; the nestling period is very short.

Eurasian Skylark
   de: Feldlerche
   fr: Alouette des champs
   es: Alondra Común
   ja: ニシヒバリ
   cn: 云雀
Alauda arvensis
Introduced.

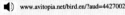 www.avitopia.net/bird.en/?aud=4427002

adult

Bulbuls - *Pycnonotidae*

The family of Bulbuls is widespread in Africa including Madagascar and in South Asia. The northern species are migratory birds. The body length ranges from 15 cm to 30 cm. They have short wings and many species have a feather crest. The Bulbuls are rather poor fliers, but move around the branches quite skillfully. Their diet is mainly vegetable, but they also eat insects. The bowl-shaped nest is built from plant material deep in the bushes. The altricial nestlings are looked after by both parents.

Red-vented Bulbul
de: Rußbülbül
fr: Bulbul à ventre rouge
es: Bulbul de Caudal Roja
ja: シリアカヒヨドリ
cn: 黑喉红臀鹎
Pycnonotus cafer
Introduced.

Photo J.M.Garg

adult

Red-whiskered Bulbul
de: Rotohrbülbül
fr: Bulbul orphée
es: Bulbul de Bigotes Rojos
ja: コウラウン
cn: 红耳鹎
Pycnonotus jocosus
Introduced.

www.avitopia.net/bird.en/?kom=4726620
www.avitopia.net/bird.en/?vid=4726620

Photo W.J.Daunicht

adult

Bush-Warblers and allies - *Scotocercidae*

The family of Bush-warblers and allies occurs in Africa, Eurasia and some islands in the Pacific. The family was recently separated from the family of Old World Warblers based on DNA testing. They are small birds between 7 cm and 15 cm in length. Some species have very short tails. The plumage shows no bright colors.

Japanese Bush Warbler
de: Japanbuschsänger
fr: Bouscarle chanteuse
es: Ruiseñor Bastardo Japonés
ja: ウグイス
cn: 日本树莺
Horornis diphone
Introduced.

adult

Reed-Warblers and allies - *Acrocephalidae*

The family of Reed-Warblers is native to Africa, Eurasia and Australia to Oceania. Many species are migratory birds. This family was only recently recognized based on DNA studies. The body size ranges from 11.5 cm to 18 cm. Almost all species have a relatively single-coloured plumage and can be better identified from their songs than from their appearance. However, the chants often contain imitations of other bird species. Most Reed-Warblers colonize wetlands or habitats near water.

Millerbird
de: Laysanrohrsänger
fr: Rousserolle obscure
es: Carricero Hawaiano
ja: ニホアヨシキリ
cn: 夏威夷苇莺
Acrocephalus familiaris
Endemic.
Critically endangered.

adult

White-eyes - *Zosteropidae*

The family of White-eyes has its distribution in Africa, South Asia and Australia to Samoa in the Pacific. Many species are endemic to small islands. The body size of these petite birds is between 10 cm and 14 cm. They have short wings with only nine hand feathers. The beak is slender, the tongue is brush-tipped and can be extended far. The appearance of the different species is often extremely similar. Many species have a conspicuous ring of tiny white feathers around their eyes. They are tree inhabitants and eat insects, fruits and nectar. They pierce fruit with their beak and pull the juice out with their tongue. The nest consists of a hanging bowl on a forked branch. The breeding season is the shortest for birds at 10 days.

adult

Japanese White-eye
> de: Japanbrillenvogel
> fr: Zostérops du Japon
> es: Ojiblanco Japonés
> ja: メジロ
> cn: 暗绿绣眼鸟
> *Zosterops japonicus*
> Introduced.

Photo Trisha Shears

Laughingthrushes and allies - *Leiothrichidae*

The family of Laughingthrushes is found in Africa and South Asia. Most of the species live in the tropics. They rarely migrate and are rather poor fliers. With almost 150 species, the family is relatively large and very diverse. It was only recently separated in the systematics from the more comprehensive family of Babblers.

adult

Hwamei
> de: Augenbrauenhäherling
> fr: Garrulaxe hoamy
> es: Tordo Jocoso Cantor
> ja: ガビチョウ
> cn: 画眉
> *Garrulax canorus*
> Introduced.

Photo Charles Lam

Greater Necklaced Laughingthrush
  de: Brustbandhäherling
  fr: Garrulaxe à plastron
  es: Tordo Jocoso Pectoral
  ja: クビワガビチョウ
  cn: 黑领噪鹛
Ianthocincla pectoralis
Introduced.

adult

Red-billed Leiothrix
  de: Sonnenvogel
  fr: Léiothrix jaune
  es: Leiothrix de Pico Rojo
  ja: ソウシチョウ
  cn: 红嘴相思鸟
Leiothrix lutea
Introduced.

adult

Flycatchers - *Muscicapidae*

The family of Flycatchers occurs in Africa, Europe and Asia. Many species are long-distance migrants. The body length ranges from 9 cm to 20 cm. Flycatchers have relatively long legs and are often strikingly colored. They mainly eat insects, but also plant-based foods.

White-rumped Shama
  de: Schamadrossel
  fr: Shama à croupion blanc
  es: Mirlo Shama Hindú
  ja: アカハラシキチョウ
  cn: 白腰鹊鸲
Copsychus malabaricus
Introduced.

adult

Thrushes - *Turdidae*

The family of Thrushes is distributed worldwide and is even found on many small islands in the Pacific, only missing in Antarctica and New Zealand. But Blackbirds and Song thrushes have been introduced there and have reproduced so much that they are now among the most common birds. Thrushes mainly feed on insects and other invertebrates, but berries also play a role in winter.

adult

Drawing F.W.Frohawk

PD Kamao
 de: Kauaiklarino
 fr: Solitaire kamao
 es: Clarín Grande de Kauai
 ja: カワイヒトリツグミ
 cn: 考岛孤鸫
Myadestes myadestinus †
Endemic.
Last seen 1987.

adult

Drawing W.J.Daunicht

AU Amaui
 de: Oahuklarino
 fr: Solitaire d'Oahu
 es: Amaui
 ja: オアフヒトリツグミ
 cn: 瓦胡岛孤鸫
Myadestes woahensis †
Endemic.
Last seen 1825.

adult

Drawing F.W.Frohawk

PD Olomao
 de: Lanaiklarino
 fr: Solitaire de Lanai
 es: Clarín de Lanai
 ja: ラナイヒトリツグミ
 cn: 拉奈孤鸫
Myadestes lanaiensis
Endemic.
Critically endangered.

Omao
  de: Hawaiiklarino
  fr: Solitaire d'Hawaï
  es: Clarín Hawaiano
  ja: ハワイツグミ
  cn: 夏威夷鸫
Myadestes obscurus
Endemic.
Vulnerable.

adult

Puaiohi
  de: Palmerklarino
  fr: Solitaire puaïohi
  es: Clarín Chico de Kauai
  ja: カウワイツグミ
  cn: 小考岛鸫
Myadestes palmeri
Endemic.
Critically endangered.

adult

Mockingbirds - *Mimidae*

The family of Mockingbirds is distributed in America from southern Canada over the Caribbean and the Galapagos Islands to Argentina. The body length is 20 cm to 30 cm. They have short wings and a long tail. Their legs are quite long. They have a large repertoire of vocalizations that can include more than a thousand song phrases. In addition, some species can imitate the voices of other birds and also technical sounds, e.g. car alarms. Most species do not fly much. The nest is a large bowl that is built in a bush or on the ground. The altricial young are looked after by both adult birds.

Northern Mockingbird
  de: Spottdrossel
  fr: Moqueur polyglotte
  es: Sinsonte Común
  ja: マネシツグミ
  cn: 小嘲鸫
Mimus polyglottos
Introduced.

adult

Starlings - *Sturnidae*

The family of Strlings was originally only distributed in the Old World, but the common star was introduced in America and is now widespread there. The body length ranges from 18 cm to 43 cm. Many species have iridescent plumage. The tail is usually short, more rarely long. Unlike thrushes, starlings do not hop, but run with alternating steps. They fly well and the formation flights of large flocks of starlings are impressive. Most species breed in tree hollows, but other nesting techniques also occur, including large community nests. Starlings are omnivores, one reason for their assertiveness as colonists.

Photo W.J.Daunicht

♂ breeding

AU Common Starling
de: Star
fr: Étourneau sansonnet
es: Estornino Pinto
ja: ホシムクドリ
cn: 紫翅椋鸟
Sturnus vulgaris
Introduced.

www.avitopia.net/bird.en/?kom=5326201

Photo W.J.Daunicht

adult

AU Common Myna
de: Hirtenmaina
fr: Martin triste
es: Mainá Común
ja: カバイロハッカ
cn: 家八哥
Acridotheres tristis
Introduced.

Mohos - *Mohoidae*

The small family of Mohos is endemic to the Hawaiian Islands. This family was only established in 2008, when it was found on the basis of DNA studies that the five species do not belong to the honeyeaters, as previously assumed. Through convergent evolution, they share many traits with honeyeaters, such as nectar nutrition, a long curved beak and a long tongue with a brush-like tip. Their body length is 20 cm to 33 cm. The Mohos are the only family of birds that became completely extinct in modern times; the Kauai Oo did not become extinct until 1987. The reason for the extinction is the habitat destruction combined with the introduction of predatory mammals and bird malaria in the Hawaiian Islands.

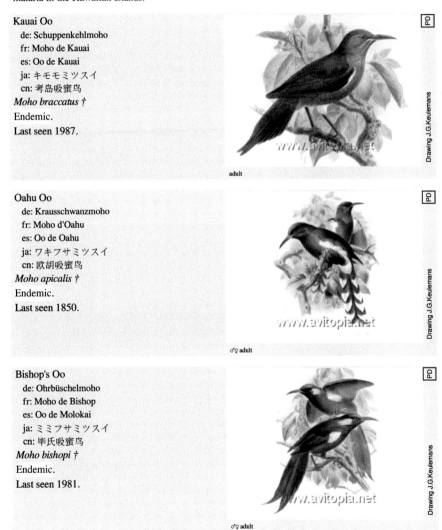

Kauai Oo
   de: Schuppenkehlmoho
   fr: Moho de Kauai
   es: Oo de Kauai
   ja: キモモミツスイ
   cn: 考岛吸蜜鸟
Moho braccatus †
Endemic.
Last seen 1987.

adult

Oahu Oo
   de: Krausschwanzmoho
   fr: Moho d'Oahu
   es: Oo de Oahu
   ja: ワキフサミツスイ
   cn: 欧胡吸蜜鸟
Moho apicalis †
Endemic.
Last seen 1850.

♂♀ adult

Bishop's Oo
   de: Ohrbüschelmoho
   fr: Moho de Bishop
   es: Oo de Molokai
   ja: ミミフサミツスイ
   cn: 毕氏吸蜜鸟
Moho bishopi †
Endemic.
Last seen 1981.

♂♀ adult

Drawing J.G.Keulemans

PD

PD Hawaii Oo
de: Prachtmoho
fr: Moho d'Hawaï
es: Oo de Hawaii
ja: ムネフサミツスイ
cn: 夏威夷吸蜜鸟
Moho nobilis †
Endemic.
Last seen 1898.

Drawing J.G.Keulemans

♂♀ adult

PD Kioea
de: Kioea
fr: Méliphage kioéa
es: Kioea
ja: ハワイカオグロミツスイ
cn: 鬓吸蜜鸟
Chaetoptila angustipluma †
Endemic.
Last seen 1900.

Drawing J.G.Keulemans

♂ adult

Tanagers - *Thraupidae*

The family of Tanagers is the second largest of the passerine birds. It has an American distribution mainly in the tropics. Their body length ranges from 9 cm to 24 cm. Their plumage is usually brightly colored, but there are also black and white species. Tangerines are omnivores. The female builds the nest and incubates, but may be fed by the male. Both parents feed the young.

PD Red-crested Cardinal
de: Graukardinal
fr: Paroare huppé
es: Cardenal de Cresta Roja
ja: コウカンチョウ
cn: 冠蜡嘴鹀
Paroaria coronata
Introduced.

Photo J.Mosesso&A.Grosse

adult

Yellow-billed Cardinal
  de: Mantelkardinal
  fr: Paroare à bec jaune
  es: Cardenal de Pico Amarillo
  ja: キバシコウカンチョウ
  cn: 黄嘴蜡嘴鹀
Paroaria capitata
Introduced.

adult

Saffron Finch
  de: Safranammer
  fr: Sicale bouton-d'or
  es: Semillero Basto
  ja: キノノジコ
  cn: 橙黄雀鹀
Sicalis flaveola
Introduced.

♂ adult

Yellow-faced Grassquit
  de: Goldbraue
  fr: Sporophile grand-chanteur
  es: Tomeguín de la Tierra
  ja: キマユクビワスズメ
  cn: 黄脸草雀
Tiaris olivaceus
Introduced.

♂ adult

Cardinals - *Cardinalidae*

The family of Cardinals is common in North and South America. They are about 12 cm to 24 cm long. They have very powerful, conical beaks and nine hand wings; the plumage has mostly bright colors in red, yellow or blue. Their habitat are bush and forest landscapes. They feed mostly on seeds.

AU Northern Cardinal
   de: Rotkardinal
   fr: Cardinal rouge
   es: Cardenal Norteño
   ja: ショウジョウコウカンチョウ
   cn: 主红雀
Cardinalis cardinalis
Introduced.

Photo W.J.Daunicht

♂ adult

New World Blackbirds - *Icteridae*

The family of New World Blackbirds is restricted to North and South America. The species are very different in size: 19 cm to 55 cm. The plumage is often black with brightly colored areas. Their food is very varied. Some species are breeding parasites, while the other species nest very differently. The hanging nests are unusual.

PD Western Meadowlark
   de: Wiesenstärling
   fr: Sturnelle de l'Ouest
   es: Turpial Gorjeador
   ja: ニシマキバドリ
   cn: 西草地鹨
Sturnella neglecta
Introduced.

Photo J.&K.Hollingsworth

adult

S2.0 Eastern Meadowlark
   de: Lerchenstärling
   fr: Sturnelle des prés
   es: Turpial Oriental
   ja: ヒガシマキバドリ
   cn: 东草地鹨
Sturnella magna
Introduced.

Photo Dominic Sherony

adult

Finches - *Fringillidae*

The family of Finches is widespread worldwide except for Australia and some oceanic islands. The body length is between 11 cm and 22 cm. They eat seeds and buds, insects almost only during the breeding season. The nest is built by the female from twigs, grass, moss and lichen in the form of a padded bowl.

Poo-uli
  de: Poo-Uli
  fr: Po-o-uli masqué
  es: Puli
  ja: カオグロハワイミツスイ
  cn: 毛岛蜜雀
Melamprosops phaeosoma †
Endemic.
Last seen 2004.

adult

Akikiki
  de: Akikiki
  fr: Grimpeur de Kauai
  es: Akikiki
  ja: カウアイキバシリ
  cn: 考岛悬木雀
Oreomystis bairdi
Endemic.
Critically endangered.

♂ adult

Oahu Alauahio
  de: Oahuastläufer
  fr: Grimpeur d'Oahu
  es: Alauajio de Oahu
  ja: キバシリハワイミツスイ
  cn: 瓦岛管舌雀
Paroreomyza maculata
Endemic.
Critically endangered.

♂ adult

♂ adult

PD **Kakawahie**
   de: Kakawahie
   fr: Grimpeur de Molokai
   es: Kakawajie
   ja: モロカイキバシリ
   cn: 莫岛管舌雀
Paroreomyza flammea †
Endemic.
Last seen 1963.

Drawing J.G.Keulemans

♂ adult

PD **Maui Alauahio**
   de: Mauiastläufer
   fr: Grimpeur de Maui
   es: Alauajio de Maui
   ja: マウイキバシリ
   cn: 毛岛管舌雀
Paroreomyza montana
Endemic.
Endangered.

Drawing J.G.Keulemans

♂ adult

PD **Palila**
   de: Palila
   fr: Psittirostre palila
   es: Palila
   ja: キムネハワイマシコ
   cn: 黄胸管舌雀
Loxioides bailleui
Endemic.
Critically endangered.

Photo J.Jeffrey

♂ adult

PD **Laysan Finch**
   de: Laysangimpel
   fr: Psittirostre de Laysan
   es: Certiola de Laysan
   ja: レイサンハワイマシコ
   cn: 莱岛拟管舌雀
Telespiza cantans
Endemic.
Vulnerable.

Photo unknown

Nihoa Finch
de: Nihoagimpel
fr: Psittirostre de Nihoa
es: Certiola de Nihoa
ja: ニホアハワイマシコ
cn: 尼岛拟管舌雀
Telespiza ultima
Endemic.
Critically endangered.

♂ adult

Grosbeak Finch
de: Konagimpel
fr: Psittirostre à gros bec
es: Kona
ja: ハワイマシコ
cn: 科纳松雀
Chloridops kona †
Endemic.
Last seen 1894.

♂ adult

Lesser Koa-Finch
de: Goldkopf-Koagimpel
fr: Petit Psittirostre
es: Koa Menor
ja: ヒメコアハワイマシコ
cn: 黄头拟管舌鸟
Rhodacanthis flaviceps †
Endemic.
Last seen 1891.

♂ adult

Greater Koa-Finch
de: Orangebrust-Koagimpel
fr: Psittirostre de Palmer
es: Koa Mayor
ja: コアハワイマシコ
cn: 大管鸹
Rhodacanthis palmeri †
Endemic.
Last seen 1896.

♂ adult

♂ adult

PD Ula-ai-hawane
  de: Kohala-Kleidervogel
  fr: Ciridopse d'Anna
  es: Ulaai-hawane
  ja: ウラアイハワネ
  cn: 安娜黑领雀
Ciridops anna †
Endemic.
Last seen 1937.

adult

PD Akohekohe
  de: Akohekohe
  fr: Palmérie huppée
  es: Akojekoje
  ja: カンムリハワイミツスイ
  cn: 冠旋蜜雀
Palmeria dolei
Endemic.
Critically endangered.

♂ adult

PD Laysan Honeycreeper
  de: Laysanapapane
  fr: Picchion de Laysan
  es: Apapane de Laysan
  ja: レッドレイサンミツスイ
  cn: 莱岛蜜雀
Himatione fraithii †
Endemic.

♂ adult

PD Apapane
  de: Apapane
  fr: Picchion cramoisi
  es: Apapane
  ja: アカハワイミツスイ
  cn: 白臀蜜雀
Himatione sanguinea
Endemic.

Drawing J.G.Keulemans

Iiwi
  de: Iiwi
  fr: Iiwi rouge
  es: Iwi
  ja: ベニハワイミツスイ
  cn: 镰嘴管舌雀
Drepanis coccinea
Endemic.
Vulnerable.

adult

Hawaii Mamo
  de: Gelbbürzelmamo
  fr: Drépanide mamo
  es: Mamo Hawaiano
  ja: マモ
  cn: 夏威夷监督吸蜜鸟
Drepanis pacifica †
Endemic.
Last seen 1898.

♂ adult

Black Mamo
  de: Rußmamo
  fr: Drépanide noir
  es: Mamo Negro
  ja: クロハワイミツスイ
  cn: 黑监督吸蜜鸟
Drepanis funerea †
Endemic.
Last seen 1907.

adult

Ou
  de: Ou
  fr: Psittirostre psittacin
  es: Ou
  ja: キガシラハワイマシコ
  cn: 鹦嘴管舌雀
Psittirostra psittacea
Endemic.
Critically endangered.

♂ adult

adult

Lanai Hookbill
de: Lanai-Hakenschnabel
fr: Psittirostre de Munro
es: Drepano de Lanai
ja: ラナイマシコ
cn: 夏威夷钩嘴雀
Dysmorodrepanis munroi †
Endemic.
Last seen 1920.

♂ adult

Maui Parrotbill
de: Papageischnabelgimpel
fr: Psittirostre de Maui
es: Pinzón Loro de Maui
ja: オウムハシハワイマシコ
cn: 毛岛鹦嘴雀
Pseudonestor xanthophrys
Endemic.
Critically endangered.

♂ adult

Kauai Nukupuu
de: Kauai-Sichelkleidervogel
fr: Nukupuu de Kauai
es: Nukupuu de Kauai
ja: カウアイカワリハシハワイミツスイ
cn: 考艾短镰嘴雀
Hemignathus hanapepe †
Endemic.
Last seen 1899.

♂ adult

Oahu Nukupuu
de: Oahu-Sichelkleidervogel
fr: Nukupuu d'Oahu
es: Nukupuu de Oahu
ja: マウイカワリハシハワイミツスイ
cn: 短镰嘴雀
Hemignathus lucidus †
Endemic.
Last seen 1860.

Maui Nukupuu
  de: Maui-Sichelkleidervogel
  fr: Nukupuu de Maui
  es: Nukupuu de Maui
  ja: マウイカワリハシハワイミツスイ
  cn: 茂宜短镰嘴雀
Hemignathus affinis †
Endemic.
Last seen 1996.

♂ adult

Akiapolaau
  de: Akiapolaau
  fr: Hémignathe akiapolaau
  es: Akiapolau
  ja: カワリハシハワイミツスイ
  cn: 镰嘴雀
Hemignathus wilsoni
Endemic.

♂ adult

Lesser Akialoa
  de: Akialoa
  fr: Hémignathe akialoa
  es: Akialoa Menor
  ja: ユミハシハワイミツスイ
  cn: 长嘴导颚雀
Akialoa obscura †
Endemic.
Last seen 1940.

♂ adult

Oahu Akialoa
  de: Oahu-Akialoa
  fr: Akialoa d'Oahu
  es: Akialoa de Oahu
  ja: オオイミツスイ
  cn: 大绿雀
Akialoa ellisiana †
Endemic.
Last seen 1969.

♀ adult

♂ adult

PD **Stejneger's Akialoa**
de: Steijneger-Akialoa
fr: Akialoa de Kauai
es: Akialoa de Kauai
ja: カウアイミツスイ
cn: 考艾大嘴雀
Akialoa stejnegeri †
Endemic.
Last seen 1969.

Drawing J.G.Keulemans

♂ adult

PD **Maui Nui Akialoa**
de: Maui Nui Akialoa
fr: Hémignathe de Lanai
es: Akialoa de Maui Nui
ja: マウイ・ヌイイミツスイ
cn: 茂宜大嘴雀
Akialoa lanaiensis †
Endemic.
Last seen 1900.

Drawing J.G.Keulemans

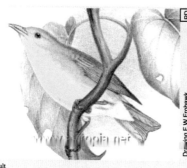

♂ adult

PD **Anianiau**
de: Anianiau
fr: Petit Amakihi
es: Anianiau
ja: コハワイミツスイ
cn: 小绿雀
Magumma parva
Endemic.
Vulnerable.

Drawing F.W.Frohawk

♂ adult

PD **Hawaii Amakihi**
de: Amakihi
fr: Amakihi d'Hawaï
es: Amakiji Hawaiano
ja: ハワイミツスイ
cn: 夏威夷绿雀
Chlorodrepanis virens
Endemic.

Drawing J.G.Keulemans

Oahu Amakihi
  de: Oahu-Amakihi
  fr: Amakihi d'Oahu
  es: Amakiji de Oahu
  ja: オハフミツスイ
  cn: 瓦岛绿雀
Chlorodrepanis flava
Endemic.
Vulnerable.

♀ adult

Kauai Amakihi
  de: Kauai-Amakihi
  fr: Amakihi de Steijneger
  es: Amakihi de Kauai
  ja: カウアイミツスイ
  cn: 考岛绿雀
Chlorodrepanis stejnegeri
Endemic.
Vulnerable.

adult

Greater Amakihi
  de: Grünrücken-Kleidervogel
  fr: Grand Amakihi
  es: Amakihi Mayor
  ja: オオハワイミツスイ
  cn: 大颚雀
Viridonia sagittirostris †
Endemic.
Last seen 1901.

♂ adult

Hawaii Creeper
  de: Hawaiiastläufer
  fr: Grimpeur d'Hawaï
  es: Trepador Hawaiano
  ja: ハワイキバシリ
  cn: 夏威夷悬木雀
Loxops mana
Endemic.
Endangered.

adult

♂ adult

PD **Akekee**
　de: Akekee
　fr: Loxopse de Kauai
　es: Akeki
　ja: コバシハワイミツスイ
　cn: 考岛管舌雀
Loxops caeruleirostris
Endemic.
Critically endangered.

Drawing J.G.Keulemans

♂ adult

PD **Hawaii Akepa**
　de: Hawaii-Akepakleidervogel
　fr: Akepa de Hawaii
　es: Akepa de Hawaii
　ja: コバシハワイミツスイ
　cn: 红管舌雀
Loxops coccineus
Endemic.
Endangered.

Drawing J.G.Keulemans

♂ adult

PD **Oahu Akepa**
　de: Oahu-Akepakleidervogel
　fr: Loxopse d'Oahu
　es: Akepa de Oahu
　ja: オアフコバシハワイミツスイ
　cn: 瓦岛红管舌雀
Loxops wolstenholmei †
Endemic.
Last seen 1890.

Drawing F.W.Frohawk

♂ adult

PD **Maui Akepa**
　de: Maui-Akepakleidervogel
　fr: Loxopse de Maui
　es: Akepa de Maui
　ja: マウイコバシハワイミツスイ
　cn: 茂宜红管舌雀
Loxops ochraceus †
Endemic.
Last seen 1988.

Drawing F.W.Frohawk

House Finch
  de: Hausgimpel
  fr: Roselin familier
  es: Carpodaco Común
  ja: メキシコマシコ
  cn: 家朱雀
Haemorhous mexicanus
Introduced.

♂ adult

Yellow-fronted Canary
  de: Mosambikgirlitz
  fr: Serin du Mozambique
  es: Canario de Frente Amarillo
  ja: キマユカナリア
  cn: 黄额丝雀
Crithagra mozambica
Introduced.

♂ adult

European Serin
  de: Girlitz
  fr: Serin cini
  es: Verdecillo
  ja: セリン
  cn: 欧洲丝雀
Serinus serinus
Introduced.

www.avitopia.net/bird.en/?vid=6129801
www.avitopia.net/bird.en/?aud=6129801

♂ adult

Atlantic Canary
  de: Kanarengirlitz
  fr: Serin des Canaries
  es: Canario Común
  ja: カナリア
  cn: 金丝雀
Serinus canaria
Introduced.

www.avitopia.net/bird.en/?vid=6129802

♂ adult

Sparrows - *Passeridae*

The sparrow family is native to Europe, Asia and Africa. However, one species managed to conquer the entire globe. The small birds are only 10 cm to 18 cm long. The conical beak indicates that they are grain eaters.

♂ adult

AU House Sparrow
    de: Haussperling
    fr: Moineau domestique
    es: Gorrión Doméstico
    ja: イエスズメ
    cn: 家麻雀
Passer domesticus
Introduced.

www.avitopia.net/bird.en/?vid=6150202
www.avitopia.net/bird.en/?aud=6150202

Photo W.J.Daunicht

Waxbills - *Estrildidae*

The family of Waxbills is found in Africa, South Asia, and Australia. They are small birds with a body length of 9 cm to 14 cm. The beak is short and strong. Most of the species are grain eaters. As a rule, they are sociable birds. The nests are messy structures that are built by both parents. The chicks' throats are often very contrasting in color. Some species are ready for breeding after just a few months.

adult

AU Lavender Waxbill
    de: Schönbürzel
    fr: Astrild queue-de-vinaigre
    es: Astrild Azul
    ja: アサギリチョウ
    cn: 淡蓝梅花雀
Estrilda caerulescens
Introduced.

Photo W.J.Daunicht

adult

PD Orange-cheeked Waxbill
    de: Orangebäckchen
    fr: Astrild à joues orange
    es: Astrild de Mejillas Anaranjadas
    ja: ホオアカカエデチョウ
    cn: 橙颊梅花雀
Estrilda melpoda
Introduced.

Drawing J.G.Keulemans

Black-rumped Waxbill
  de: Grauastrild
  fr: Astrild cendré
  es: Astrild de Lomo Negro
  ja: カエデチョウ
  cn: 黑腰梅花雀
Estrilda troglodytes
Introduced.

adult

Common Waxbill
  de: Wellenastrild
  fr: Astrild ondulé
  es: Pico de Coral
  ja: オナガカエデチョウ
  cn: 梅花雀
Estrilda astrild
Introduced.

adult

Red-cheeked Cordon-bleu
  de: Schmetterlingsastrild
  fr: Cordonbleu à joues rouges
  es: Cordón Azul de Mejillas Rojas
  ja: セイキチョウ
  cn: 红颊蓝饰雀
Uraeginthus bengalus
Introduced.

♂ adult

Red Avadavat
  de: Tigerastrild
  fr: Bengali rouge
  es: Bengalí Rojo
  ja: ベニスズメ
  cn: 红梅花雀
Amandava amandava
Introduced.

♂ adult

adult

AU African Silverbill
de: Afrikanischer Silberschnabel
fr: Capucin bec-d'argent
es: Capuchino Africano
ja: アフリカギンバシ
cn: 银嘴文鸟
Euodice cantans
Introduced.

Photo W.J.Daunicht

adult

AU Scaly-breasted Munia
de: Muskatamadine
fr: Capucin damier
es: Capuchino Nutmeg
ja: シマキンパラ
cn: 斑文鸟
Lonchura punctulata
Introduced.

Photo W.J.Daunicht

adult

PD Chestnut Munia
de: Schwarzkopfnonne
fr: Capucin à tête noire
es: Capuchino Castaño
ja: ミナミギンパラ
cn: 栗腹文鸟
Lonchura atricapilla
Introduced.

Drawing A.Thorburn

adult

AU Java Sparrow
de: Javareisfink
fr: Padda de Java
es: Gorrión Javanés
ja: ブンチョウ
cn: 禾雀
Lonchura oryzivora
Introduced.
Vulnerable.

Photo W.J.Daunicht

www.avitopia.net/bird.en/?vid=6203231

Index of English Names

Index of Scientific Names

Additional Copyright Terms

Please note the following copyright terms applying to the individual fotos, drawings, and grafics contained in this e-book:

As far as known, the names of the authors (photographers, graphic artists and other creators) of the individual photos, drawings, graphics, maps and other works are placed directly next to the respective images (Attribution).

Moreover, every photo, drawing, graphic, map and each other work is labeled with an abbreviation that refers to the license under which the work has been reproduced here. These abbreviations mean:

Made in the USA
Columbia, SC
06 December 2022